ISAAC ASIMOV'S
LIBRARY OF THE UNIVERSE

THE SPACE SPOTTER'S GUIDE

by Isaac Asimov

DELL YEARLING NONFICTION

Published by
Dell Publishing
a division of
Bantam Doubleday Dell Publishing Group, Inc.
666 Fifth Avenue
New York, New York 10103

Special thanks to Julian Baum and Richard Baum.

Consultant: Fran Millhouser

ISBN: 0-440-40388-X

Reprinted by arrangement with Gareth Stevens, Inc.

Printed in the United States of America
March 1991

10 9 8 7 6 5 4 3 2 1

CONTENTS

Nowadays, we have seen planets up close, all the way to distant Neptune. We have mapped Venus through its clouds. We have seen the rings around Neptune and the ice volcanoes on Triton, one of Neptune's moons. We have detected strange objects no one knew anything about until recently: quasars, pulsars, black holes. We have learned amazing facts about how the Universe was born and have some ideas about how it may die. Nothing can be more astonishing and more interesting.

Of course, few of us will ever be able to go out into space. And few of us even have the advanced instruments needed to make interesting new discoveries about the Universe. But we can all look at the stars with the help of binoculars or small telescopes in places away from the bright lights and dust of a big city.

In this book, you will learn how to spot some of the wonders of our Solar system, our Galaxy, and beyond!

Isaac Asimov —

Our Changing Sky

The sky changes as we watch! Through the night, we see stars rise and set, turning in large circles about a spot in the sky near Polaris. That's because Earth is turning on its axis.

Polaris is also called the North Star, because it is almost directly above Earth's North Pole. Because of this, it doesn't move, but always stays in the north.

From night to night, the sky shifts, too. A pattern of stars at midnight on one night won't return exactly until a whole year has passed. So the patterns change with the seasons. That's because Earth revolves around the Sun.

Left: In this time-lapse photograph, the Sun, Moon, and stars appear to wheel across the sky, an illusion caused by the spinning planet on which we live.

Earth's Neighbor

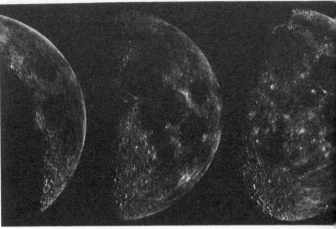

As you might guess, the brightest object in the night sky is the Moon. The Moon shines by reflected light from the Sun. When the Moon and Sun are on opposite sides of Earth, we see the Moon's lighted side as a "full Moon" shining all night.

When the Moon and Sun are on the same side of the Earth, we face the Moon's unlighted side. Perhaps we see just a bit of the lighted side as a crescent just after sunset. From night to night, the crescent gets thicker until there is a full Moon, and then thinner and thinner until there is a "new Moon."

The Moon goes around the Earth in a little less than a month. In that time, we see all its shapes, or phases, in order.

Stonehenge — a prehistoric observatory?

Before modern astronomical instruments were invented, people had their own ways of watching the stars. In England, there is a circle of large upright stones with other stones in the center. It is called Stonehenge. Some astronomers think Stonehenge might be what is left of a prehistoric observatory. Did ancient astronomers look across the stones to see where the Sun would rise at the summer solstice — or to predict lunar eclipses? We can't be sure.

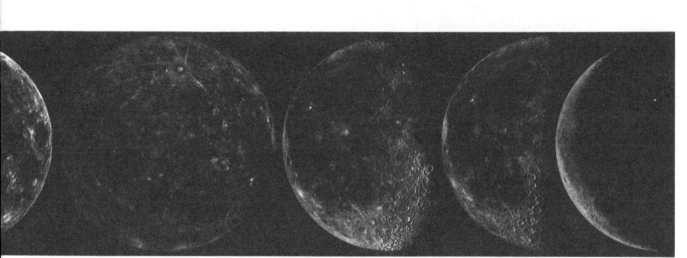

The phases of the Moon. The Moon's appearance changes as it orbits
Earth each month.

A dramatic shot of our nearest neighbor in space.

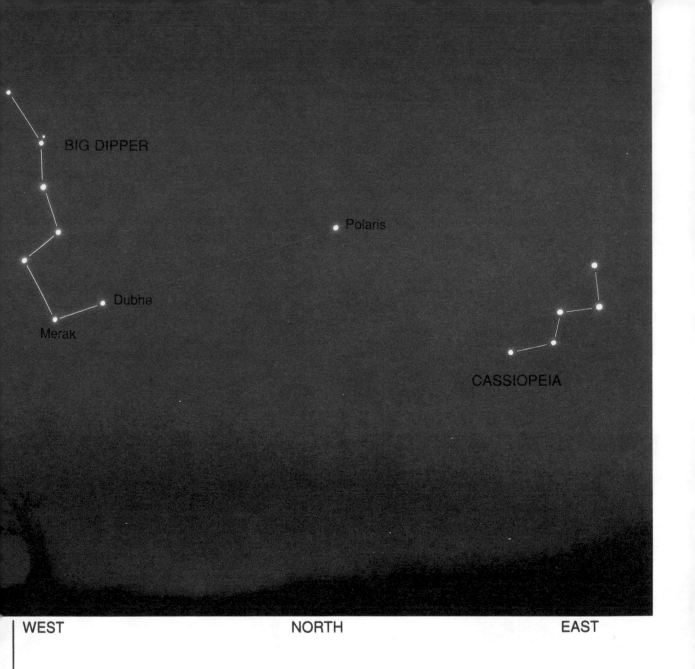

WEST   NORTH   EAST

Stars for All Seasons

From the Northern Hemisphere, we see certain patterns of
stars, or constellations, circling Polaris. They never set and are
always visible. There are some stars that circle a point above
the South Pole, opposite Polaris. A constellation called the
Southern Cross, or Crux, points to the place the southern stars
circle around. But in the Northern Hemisphere, we never see
this part of the sky.

The chief northern constellation is Ursa Major, the Great Bear. This constellation includes the seven stars of the Big Dipper. The two stars at the bowl end of the dipper are called the "pointers." Follow an imaginary line through them to find Polaris. On the other side of Polaris from the Big Dipper are five stars in a "W" shape. This constellation is Cassiopeia (pronounced cass-ee-o-PEEH-uh), the Queen.

Left: The Big Dipper and Cassiopeia are visible all year round in the Northern Hemisphere.

Below: If you looked in the northern sky at the same time each night, you'd see the Big Dipper and Cassiopeia slowly chase each other around Polaris, the North Star.

WINTER

SPRING

SUMMER

AUTUMN

The Stars of Spring

For the next eight pages, each sky picture points you toward the south. As you face south, imagine that the top of the picture is folded toward you and passes over your head. The bottom of the picture would then be south, and the top would be north.

As you face south in the spring and look way up over your head, the Big Dipper will stretch across the sky above you. If you follow the curve of the handle of the Big Dipper back toward the southern part of the sky, you will come upon the constellation Boötes (pronounced bo-OH-taze), the Herdsman. One part of Boötes is Arcturus (ark-TOOR-us), which is one of the brightest stars in the spring sky.

Continue to follow the imaginary curve south, and you will come to the constellation Virgo, the Maiden, and its bright star, Spica (SPEE-kuh). To the west (right as you face south) of Virgo is the constellation Leo, the Lion, with its bright star, Regulus.

Virgo and Leo are two of the 12 constellations of the zodiac (ZO-dee-ak). The Sun, Moon, and planets travel through the zodiac as they move across the sky.

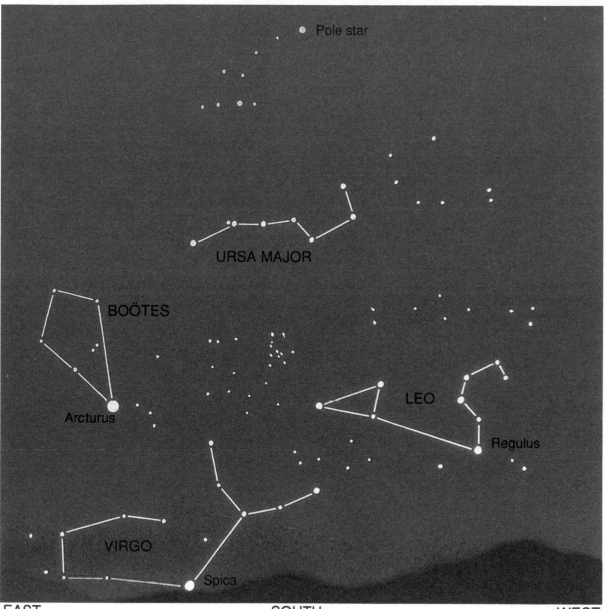

Pole star

URSA MAJOR

BOÖTES

Arcturus

LEO

Regulus

VIRGO

Spica

EAST   SOUTH   WEST

Above: With the Big Dipper overhead, look for Boötes and the bright star Arcturus in the east, Virgo in the south, and Leo in the west.

Right: the Zodiac of Dendera — a star map of ancient Egypt.

The Stars of Summer

One of the easiest constellations to spot in the summer sky is Sagittarius (saj-it-TAIR-ee-us), the Archer. Its outline looks like a teapot in the southern sky.

The Milky Way, a band of foggy light that encircles the sky, passes through Sagittarius and is brightest there. If you use a small telescope, you can see many stars in the Milky Way.

To the west, right of Sagittarius as you face south, is a curve of stars. This constellation is Scorpius (SCORE-peeh-us), the Scorpion, with its bright red star, Antares (an-TAR-eze). Antares is a red giant, hundreds of times wider than our Sun.

Over your head as you face south, and halfway between Sagittarius and Polaris, is Lyra (LIE-ruh), the Lyre, with its bright star, Vega (VAY-guh). To the east of Lyra is Cygnus (SIG-nus), the Swan, with its bright star, Deneb (DEN-eb). Halfway between Deneb and Sagittarius is the bright star Altair, in Aquila (ACK-wuh-luh), the Eagle. The three stars Vega, Deneb, and Altair form a star pattern we call the Summer Triangle.

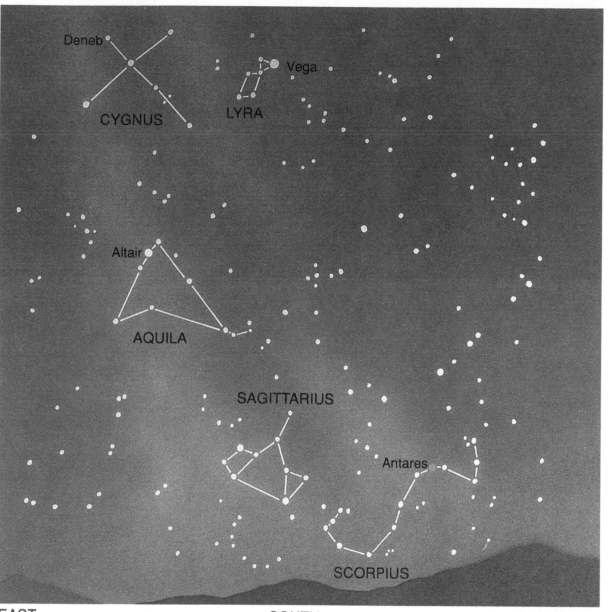

Deneb

Vega

CYGNUS

LYRA

Altair

AQUILA

SAGITTARIUS

Antares

SCORPIUS

EAST   SOUTH   WEST

Above: Lyra shines overhead, with Cygnus off to
the east and Aquila to the south. Farther south and
west lie Sagittarius and Scorpius.

Right: Sagittarius, the Archer.

The Stars of Autumn

The constellation Pegasus, the Flying Horse, is high up in the autumn sky (nearly overhead as you face south). Its four bright stars form the Square of Pegasus. Immediately to its northeast (above and to the left of Pegasus), is Andromeda (an-DROM-uh-duh), the Chained Maiden. Andromeda is exciting because within it, you can just barely spot a small, foggy patch of light.

If we look at this patch through a telescope, it turns out to be a huge collection of stars called the Andromeda Galaxy.

To the southeast of Pegasus (lower left as you face south) is Cetus (SEE-tus), the Whale, which has a rather dim star that is variable. A variable star grows brighter, then dimmer. When astronomers first saw this star, this changing brightness seemed so unusual that they named the star Mira (MEER-uh), which means "wonderful."

How far away can we see?

The most distant object we can clearly see without a telescope is the Andromeda Galaxy. It looks like a dim, fuzzy star, but it is really a galaxy larger than our own. It is about 2.3 million light-years away. But we can see still farther with a telescope. For instance, the nearest quasar is about a billion light-years away, and others might be as many as 17 billion light-years away. Astronomers don't expect to see many things much farther away than that!

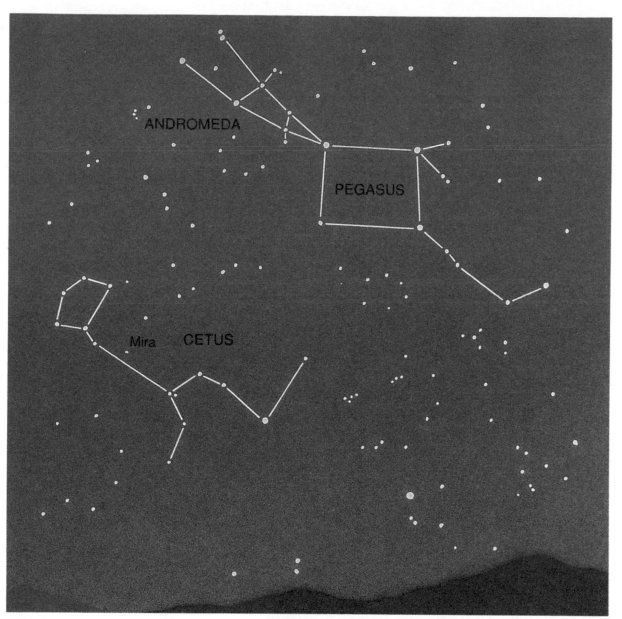

ANDROMEDA

PEGASUS

Mira   CETUS

EAST   SOUTH   WEST

Above: Three large
constellations dominate the
autumn sky — Pegasus,
Andromeda, and Cetus.

Right: Andromeda contains
the farthest object visible to
the unaided eye — galaxy
M31, the Andromeda Galaxy.
Its light has traveled for over
two million years before
reaching us!

The Stars of Winter

In the cold winter sky, you can see Orion (oh-RI-un), the Hunter. This beautiful constellation can help you find other star groups in the winter sky. On Orion's northeastern edge (the upper left, as you face south) is the huge red giant star called Betelgeuse (BEE-tul-jooz). Orion's southwestern edge (lower right) is marked by Rigel (RI-jel), a star about 55,000 times brighter than our Sun.

Between these two bright stars is a row of three stars, Orion's belt. Below the belt is another row of stars, Orion's sword. The middle "star" of the sword is actually a huge cloud of gas and dust called the Orion Nebula. Orion's belt points down and to the left (southeast) at the bright star Sirius (SIR-ee-us), in Canis Major, the Great Dog. Sirius is the brightest star visible from Earth — not counting the Sun, of course!

The belt also points up and to the right (northwest) toward Aldebaran (al-DEB-air-en), the brightest star in Taurus, the Bull.

Did Sirius change color?

Some ancient writers describe Sirius as red. But we can see that Sirius is a brilliant <u>white</u> star. Could it have been red in ancient times and have turned white? Astronomers don't see how. Of course, the ancient Egyptians watched Sirius rise with the Sun so they would know when the Nile River would flood. When it rose, Sirius might have looked reddish, just as the Sun does. That might have started people thinking of Sirius as red. But we can't be sure!

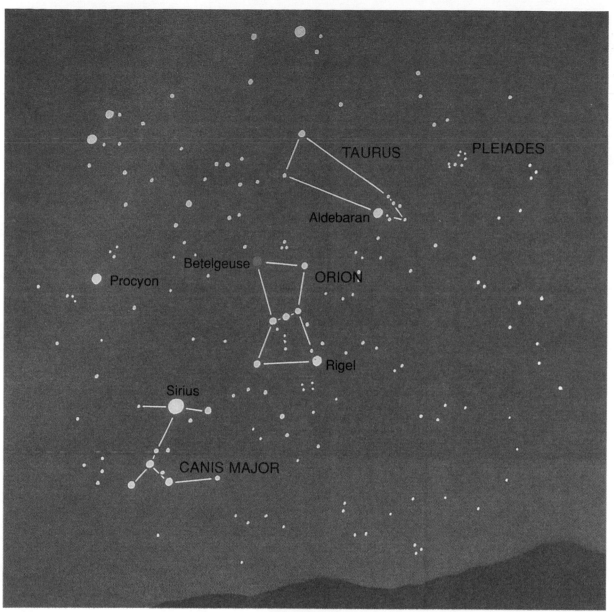

TAURUS

PLEIADES

Aldebaran

Betelgeuse

Procyon

ORION

Rigel

Sirius

CANIS MAJOR

EAST   SOUTH   WEST

Above: Sirius, the brightest star in the sky, gleams in the southeast. Rigel and Aldebaran, nearly due south, shine higher up.

Right: With binoculars, you may notice that the middle star of the three hanging off Orion's belt looks fuzzy and greenish. It's really the Orion Nebula, a giant gas cloud in which stars are born.

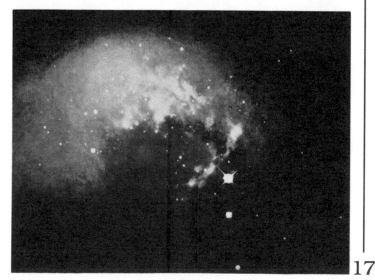

Sky Wanderers

Not all the objects in the sky turn in
one group or follow the same path.

The Moon moves across the sky
through the 12 constellations of the
zodiac, making its complete circle in a
little less than a month. The Sun
moves along the same path. But it
moves much more slowly, staying in
each constellation of the zodiac for
one month and making its complete
circuit in a year.

Five bright, starlike objects —
Mercury, Venus, Mars, Jupiter, and
Saturn — also move along the zodiac.
These also take different lengths of
time to move across the sky. For
example, Jupiter takes almost 12 years
to circle the sky, while Saturn takes
more than 29.

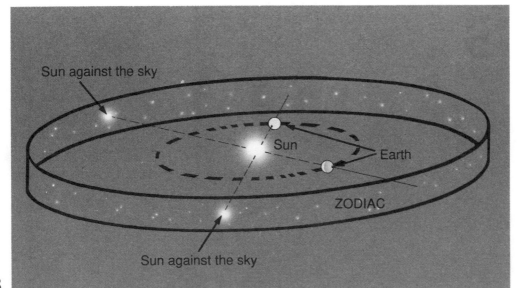

Sun against the sky

Sun

Earth

ZODIAC

Sun against the sky

Above: the zodiac constellations. Clockwise from the top: Leo, Cancer, Gemini, Taurus, Aries, Pisces, Aquarius, Capricorn, Sagittarius, Scorpius, Libra, and Virgo.

Left: As Earth moves in its yearly orbit around the Sun, it is the Sun that appears to move against the background of stars in the sky. The constellations it moves through make up the zodiac.

A naked-eye view of brilliant Venus and dim Mercury as they line up
with a crescent Moon.

Venus and Mercury

Venus and Mercury are closer to the Sun than we are. For that reason, we always see them near the Sun. Naturally, we can't see them in the daytime.

But when the Sun sets, Venus is sometimes in the western sky as the brilliant Evening Star, setting a couple of hours later. When it is on the other side of the Sun, it shines in the eastern sky before dawn as the Morning Star.

Mercury is even closer to the Sun, but it is dimmer, so it is harder to observe. But through a telescope, you can see that both Mercury and Venus show phases, just as the Moon does.

Two space-probe photos. Above: The clouds of Venus reflect sunlight, making the planet appear very bright. Below: Mercury, with its barren, cratered surface, is much harder to see.

Jupiter (upper right) and Venus, together with a young
Moon. Right: Mars through a large telescope.

The Outer Planets

Mars, Jupiter, and Saturn are all farther from the Sun than Earth is. They can all shine in the midnight sky. Since we always see their sunlit portions, they are always "full" when we see them.

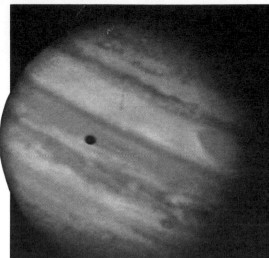

Jupiter, the largest known planet.

Mars is reddish in color. Jupiter and Saturn are giant planets. Through the telescope, you can see Jupiter as a small globe, along with its four large satellites. Saturn has a bright ring of ice and rock particles circling it, and it is one of the most beautiful sights in the heavens.

There are still farther planets: Uranus, Neptune, and Pluto. You can see Uranus and Neptune easily with a small telescope, but you need a large one to see Pluto.

Saturn, the ringed beauty.

How far is "far" in space?

The farthest known planet in our Solar system is Pluto. Traveling at 186,000 miles (300,000 km) a second, light takes about 5 1/2 hours to reach us from Pluto. The nearest star, Alpha Centauri, is so far away that its light takes 4.3 years to reach us. We say it is 4.3 light-years away. Other stars, of course, are much farther, and our Milky Way Galaxy, a huge collection of stars shaped like a pinwheel, is about 100,000 light-years from end to end.

Choosing a Telescope

At first, a good pair of binoculars will be fine for viewing the heavens. You will be able to see great views of the Milky Way and stars ten times too faint for your eyes alone. But you can do all this and more with a telescope!

Telescopes come in two varieties: refracting and reflecting. Refractors use lenses to concentrate the light. Reflectors use curved mirrors to concentrate the light.

Whichever type of telescope you choose will enable you to see the stunning sights overhead. You can watch for artificial satellites, study the surface of the Moon, and see comets in great detail.

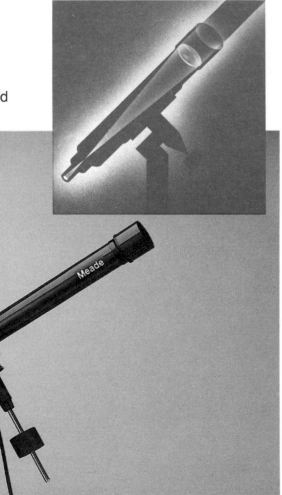

In a refracting telescope, a large lens collects and focuses light to the eyepiece.

In a reflecting telescope, a large mirror bounces and focuses light onto a smaller mirror, which bounces it into the eyepiece.

The tiniest stars pack a powerful punch!

Stars like Betelgeuse are hundreds of times wider than the Sun. Others are pushed together so tightly that they are smaller than our Earth, but contain as much matter as the Sun. One type is white-hot, so it is called a white dwarf. But even tighter, smaller stars are possible. If all the particles in our Sun were pushed together until they touched, the Sun would be only eight miles (13 km) across! Stars like this, called neutron stars, actually exist.

25

Viewing Deep Space

The stars we see with our eyes alone are only the nearest stars. With telescopes, we can see objects farther off.

There are star clusters, each of which may contain thousands of stars. The largest star cluster is in the constellation of Hercules.

You can also use a telescope to see distant galaxies that lie far beyond our Milky Way. Each contains hundreds of billions of stars. The Andromeda Galaxy is one of the closest. Some of these galaxies look like oval bits of fog. Some look like pinwheels and are called spiral galaxies.

Even a small telescope will give you an idea of the vastness of the Universe.

From Earth, the spiral Whirlpool Galaxy (M51) looks like a fuzzy pinwheel.

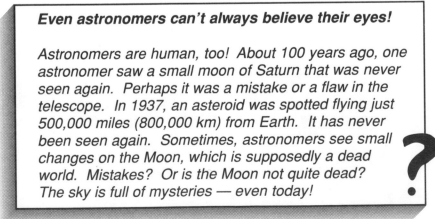

Even astronomers can't always believe their eyes!

Astronomers are human, too! About 100 years ago, one astronomer saw a small moon of Saturn that was never seen again. Perhaps it was a mistake or a flaw in the telescope. In 1937, an asteroid was spotted flying just 500,000 miles (800,000 km) from Earth. It has never been seen again. Sometimes, astronomers see small changes on the Moon, which is supposedly a dead world. Mistakes? Or is the Moon not quite dead? The sky is full of mysteries — even today!

The Helix Nebula is a faint shell of gas blown off an aging star. Right: Our neighbor, the Andromeda Galaxy. Are there astronomers looking back at us — and seeing the Milky Way as it looked over two million years ago?

Fact File: Constellations in the Southern Hemisphere

Many of the constellations that we in the Northern Hemisphere see are named after the gods and heroes of ancient Greek mythology, or after objects that were in common use even in ancient times.

But what about the stars that people in the Southern Hemisphere see? Not many people in the Northern Hemisphere thought or cared about the Southern Hemisphere sky until late in the 16th century, when explorers needed to map the southern sky so they could navigate their ships at night.

So when astronomers did give names to the constellations of the Southern Hemisphere, they did not use names from ancient myths. Instead, they named the constellations after animals found in explorers' travels and instruments used to find their way amid the sea and stars.

Here is a file of just a few of the many constellations you can spot in the skies of the Southern Hemisphere.

When humans travel to distant planets, stars, and galaxies in the future, the star patterns they see will be different from the constellations we know. What beings or things will they name <u>their</u> constellations after?

Here is a view of the Southern Hemisphere sky showing some of the constellations featured in the chart on the next page. Also shown are the Southern Cross, or Crux, which is a key constellation for finding one's way around the sky south of the equator; the Small Magellanic Cloud and the Large Magellanic Cloud, which are two small neighboring galaxies; the Coal Sack, a dark, dusty nebula; and a portion of our very own Galaxy, the Milky Way.

Name of Constellation	Description	Named by	Year
Dorado Tucana Apus	Goldfish Toucan Bird of Paradise	Johann Bayer (Germany)	1603
Circinus Horologium Antlia Telescopium	Compasses Clock Air Pump Telescope	Nicholas Louis Lacaille (France)	1750s

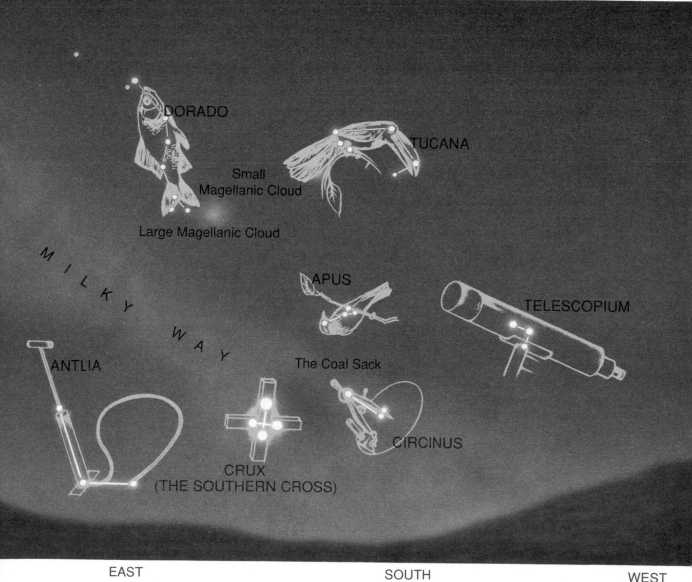

More Books About Astronomy

Here are more books that contain information about astronomy. If you are interested in them, check your library or bookstore.

Ancient Astronomy. Asimov (Gareth Stevens)
Astronomy Basics. Litpak (Prentice-Hall)
Far Out: How to Create Your Own Star World. West (Carolrhoda Books)
Find the Constellations. Rey (Houghton Mifflin)
Galaxies. Simon (Morrow)
Night Sky. Barrett (Franklin Watts)
Night Sky Book. Jobb (Little, Brown)
Peterson First Guide to Astronomy. Pasachoff (Houghton Mifflin)
Sun Dogs and Shooting Stars: A Skywatcher's Calendar. Branley (Houghton Mifflin)

Places to Visit

You can map the planets and stars without leaving Earth. Here are some museums, observatories, planetariums, and centers where you can stargaze to your heart's content.

McDonald Observatory
Austin, Texas

Gordon MacMillan Southam Observatory
Vancouver, British Columbia

Hayden Planetarium — American Museum
New York, New York

Star Theatre — Edmonton Space Sciences Centre
Edmonton, Alberta

Dow Planetarium
Montreal, Quebec

Adler Planetarium
Chicago, Illinois

For More Information About Astronomy

Here are some people you can write to or call for more information about astronomy. Be sure to tell them exactly what you want to know about or see. Remember to include your age, full name, and address.

Astronomical "Hotline" for up-to-date descriptions of the sky:

Dial (416) 586-5751
The McLaughlin Planetarium
Toronto, Ontario

For monthly sky maps:

National Museum of Science and Technology
Astronomy Division
2380 Lancaster Road
Ottawa, Ontario K1A 0M8, Canada

For catalogs of slides, posters, and other astronomy materials:

AstroMedia Order Department
21027 Crossroads Circle
Waukesha, Wisconsin 53186

Sky Publishing Corporation
49 Bay State Road
Cambridge, Massachusetts 02238-1290

Selectory Sales
Astronomical Society of the Pacific
1290 24th Avenue
San Francisco, California 94122

Hansen Planetarium
15 South State Street
Salt Lake City, Utah 84111

Glossary

Andromeda Galaxy: a huge collection of stars in the constellation Andromeda that can be seen with a telescope.

axis: the imaginary line through the center of a planet around which the planet rotates. The axis of Earth extends from the North Pole to the South Pole.

billion: In this book, the number represented by 1 followed by nine zeroes — 1,000,000,000. In some places, such as the United Kingdom (Britain), this number is called "a thousand million." In these places, one billion would then be represented by 1 followed by *12* zeroes — 1,000,000,000,000: a million million, known as a trillion in North America.

constellation: a grouping of stars in the sky that seems to trace out a familiar pattern, figure, or symbol. Constellations are often named after that which they are thought to resemble.

galaxy: any of the many large groupings of stars, gas, and dust that exist in the Universe. Our Galaxy is known as the Milky Way.

moon: a natural satellite revolving around a planet.

"new Moon": that crescent-shaped bit of the lighted side of the Moon that we see as the Moon begins a new cycle; also, the stage of the Moon during which it is invisible from Earth.

Northern Hemisphere: the half of Earth north of the equator.

observatory: a building or other structure designed for watching and recording celestial objects or events.

phases: the periods when Venus, Mercury, and our Moon are partly lit by the Sun. It takes about one month for Earth's Moon to progress from full Moon to full Moon.

"pointers": the two stars at the bowl end of the Big Dipper that point toward the North Star, or Polaris.

prehistoric: the period in history before writing was invented.

pulsar: a neutron star sending out rapid pulses of light or other radiation.

quasar: a "quasi-stellar," or "star-like," core of a galaxy that may have a large black hole at its center.

red giant: a huge star that develops when the hydrogen in an aging star runs low and the extra heat makes the star expand. The outer layers then change to a cool red.

reflector: a type of telescope that uses curved mirrors to concentrate light.

refractor: a type of telescope that uses lenses to concentrate light.

revolve: to go around completely or circle, as Earth revolves around the Sun.

Stonehenge: a place in southwestern England that may have been an ancient observatory.

summer solstice: in the Northern Hemisphere, the time of year, around June 22, when the Sun is highest in the sky. The summer solstice marks the official start of summer. The winter solstice, when the Sun is lowest in the sky, is around December 22. This marks the start of winter.

Universe: all existing things, including Earth and the Sun, Solar system, galaxies, and all that which is or may be beyond.

variable star: a star whose light grows brighter, then dimmer.

white dwarf: the small white-hot body that remains when a star like our Sun collapses.

zodiac: the band of 12 constellations across the sky that represents the paths of the Sun, the Moon, Mercury, Venus, Mars, Jupiter, and Saturn.

Index

The publishers wish to thank the following for permission to reproduce copyright material: front cover, p. 27 (upper), © Anglo-Australian Telescope Board, David Malin, 1979; p. 4, © Anglo-Australian Telescope Board, David Malin, 1980; pp. 6-7, Lick Observatory Photographs; pp. 7 (lower), 20, 22 (upper), © Frank Zullo; pp. 8, 9, 10, 11 (upper), 12, 13 (upper), 14, 15 (upper), 16, 17, © Julian Baum, 1988; p. 11 (lower), photograph courtesy of Julian Baum; p. 13 (lower), Science Photo Library; p. 15 (lower), National Optical Astronomy Observatories; pp. 17 (lower), 21 (lower), 23 (both), 26, courtesy of NASA; pp. 18-19, © Brad Greenwood, courtesy of Hansen Planetarium; pp. 19 (lower), 24 (upper), 25 (lower), © Matthew Groshek; p. 21 (upper), Jet Propulsion Laboratory; p. 22 (lower), © California Institute of Technology, 1965; pp. 24 (lower), 25 (upper), Meade Instruments; p. 27 (lower), © California Institute of Technology, 1959; p. 28, © Julian Baum and Matthew Groshek, 1988.